I Feel...
MEH

Words and pictures by

DJ Corchin

Sometimes I feel **meh.**

And I don't want to **play**.

I don't want to **read**

and have nothing to **say**.

You might bring me flowers to **brighten** my day,

But I'm neither **happy** nor **sad**,

I'm just kind of **gray**.

I don't want to **jump**.

I don't want to **sing**.

I don't want to **sculpt** a **weird**-looking thing.

I don't want to **talk** about your collection of string.

And I don't really **care** about the weather in spring.

Sometimes people ask how I'm **feeling** inside.

I'm not really sure,
I just can't **decide**.

So I think really **hard** of all the things I could do.

To get out of this **slump**.

And out of my **room.**

I might **fly** a kite to get some **fresh** air.

Or **draw** secret plans.

For my new **secret** lair.

I could **practice** my music on my super **loud** snare.

Or rehearse a new dance
with **gusto** and **flair**.

There's so **much** to do.

And so **much** to see.

There's so **much** to eat.

And so **much** to be.

When I'm feeling **meh**,
I know it's not **wrong**.

But I shouldn't **wait** to have **fun** for too long.

I Feel...
MEH

I just feel, ya know, meh. What can I do?

When someone asks you how you feel, sometimes the answer is just, "Meh." You don't feel one particular way and you don't want to do anything. Once in a while, it's ok to feel that way, we all do. But it's not ok to feel meh for too long. Here's some suggestions to come out a of a meh funk.

Plan a Non-Meh Day

1. Grab a piece of lined notebook paper.

2. On the top, write "A Non-Meh Day."

3. On the left side, you can list each hour of the day.

4. Next to each hour, write down only super fun things to do with someone else.

5. Be sure to fill the entire day from the time you wake up until bedtime.

6. Make sure you plan a fun activity for meals too!

7. With your friends, family, or trusted adults, pick a day when you can use your plan!

Switcheroo Story

1. Think about a time when you enjoyed going on an adventure with people you love. For example, visiting a zoo, or a museum, or even a hike in the woods. No adventure? No problem! Just think about all the things that happened to you since you woke up today.

2. Write down all the friends or family that were with you.

3. List all the different moments that happened, such as finding a rock, driving around, or seeing an animal.

4. Next to all the people and moments you've listed, switch up their names and even what type of creature or person they are. For example, your aunt Lucy could be Lucielle the Griffin. Your dog Fido could be Fidolf the Great Warrior. Finding a rock could be finding a magical, glowing gem.

5. Now write the entire story using the switched names and characters and see what amazing creation you come up with.

Make a Meh Scale

Sometimes just knowing and being aware of how meh we actually feel can help us with what to do next.

1. Using a large poster board or the side of a cardboard box, cut out a long rectangle.

2. Find a large clothespin and paint or color it gray. If you don't have a clothespin, you can use a paper clip.

3. Measure out five smaller rectangles on the one you cut out and draw a line dividing them spaced out evenly.

4. From left to right, write in each rectangle:

   Super Mega Meh

   Really Meh

   Meh

   Meh-ish

   Totally Not Meh

5. You can color or decorate each rectangle however you want.

6. Tape up the Meh Scale behind your door or on a wall.

7. Move the clothespin or clip to the rectangle that best fits your level of meh.

8. You can even talk about it with a trusted friend or family member whenever you move the clip.

Music, Meh, and Me.

1. Listen to some of your favorite music that has words in it.

2. In a small notebook or sketchbook, write down phrases that make you feel a specific emotion.

   Put one phrase on the bottom each page. Add the song's title as well.

3. Draw an I Feel... face that shows how the phrase makes you feel on each page.

4. You can take each page and organize the phrases by different feelings.

5. When you're feeling meh, pick a song based on the feeling you get from it.

Meh. Me. Activities.

When you don't feel like doing anything, try doing small amounts of lots of things!

1. Think through all the different types of activities you can do such as dancing, playing basketball, drawing, playing piano, singing, etc.

2. Write them down on different index cards (one on each card).

3. Set a time for five minutes and pick a random card, place it back in the pile, then start the timer and do the activity written on the card.

4. Every five minutes, repeat step three for one hour.

It is ALWAYS OK to ask someone for help when you are feeling bad.

The I Feel... Children's Series is a resource created to assist in discussions about emotional awareness.

Please seek the help of a trained mental healthcare professional and start a discussion today.

To Kim

Published by Sourcebooks eXplore, an imprint of Sourcebooks Kids
P.O. Box 4410, Naperville, Illinois 60567-4410
(630) 961-3900
sourcebookskids.com

Originally published in 2016 in the United States of America by The phazelFOZ Company, LLC.

Library of Congress Cataloging-in-Publication Data is on file with the publisher.

Source of Production: 1010 Printing Asia Limited, North Point, Hong Kong, China
Date of Production: September 2020
Run Number: 5019345

Printed and bound in China.
OGP 10 9 8 7 6 5 4 3 2 1